Sherry:

It's been a pleasure living here

and knowing you, thank you SO much!

Lixin

19th, Oct, 2008

CAT GETTING OUT OF A BAG
AND OTHER OBSERVATIONS

JEFFREY BROWN

CHRONICLE BOOKS
SAN FRANCISCO

LIBRARY OF CONGRESS CATALOGING-IN-PUBLICATION DATA AVAILABLE.

ISBN: 0-8118-5822-7
ISBN-13: 978-0-8118-5822-9

MANUFACTURED IN HONG KONG.

10 9 8 7 6 5 4 3

CHRONICLE BOOKS LLC
680 SECOND STREET
SAN FRANCISCO CA 94107

www.chroniclebooks.com

THIS IS ME (TYPICAL PHONE CALL WITH CAT OWNER)

> OOH! YOU SHOULD SEE MISTY RIGHT NOW!

> SHE'S LYING ON HER BACK WITH HER HEAD UPSIDE-DOWN

> HA HA! NOW SHE'S ROLLING AROUND BATTING AT THE CHAIR!

> AND NOW SHE'S PURRING AND HOLDING THE TABLE LEG...

CATS I HAVE LIVED WITH

MISTY

OBIE

KITTY

BUDDY

ONE REASON I WROTE THIS BOOK

> HA HA!

FUNNY HOME VIDEO SHOW

REWIND

> HA HA HA!

> WHAT'S SO FUNNY!

> CHECK OUT THIS CAT

REWIND

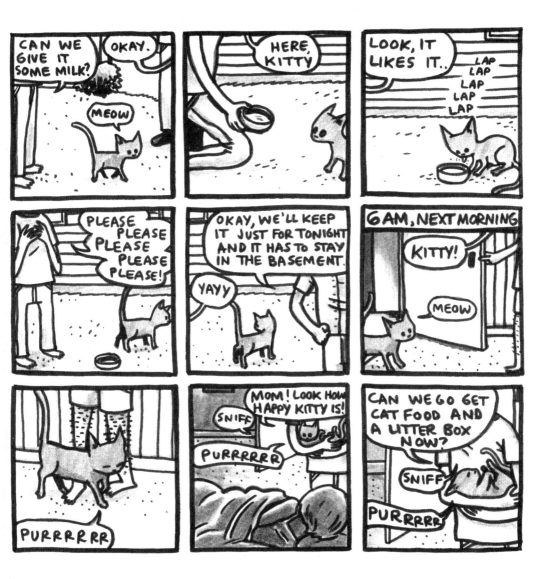

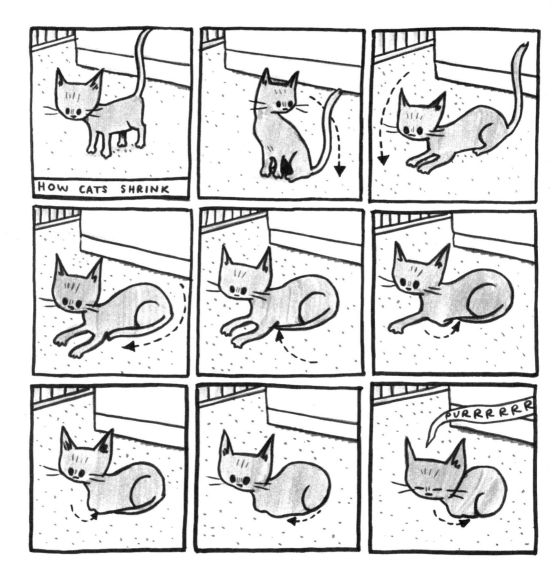

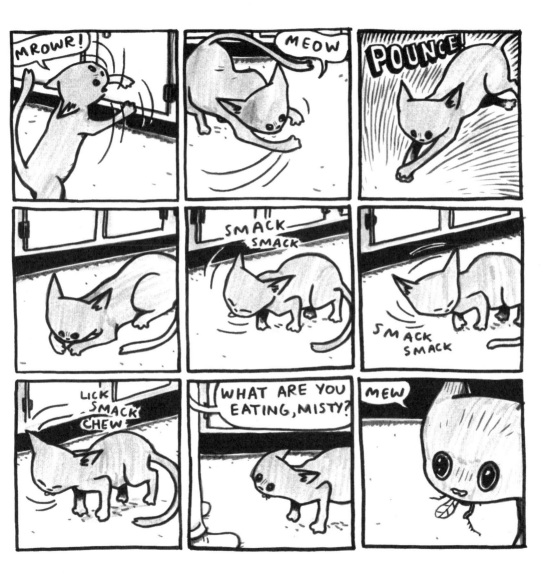

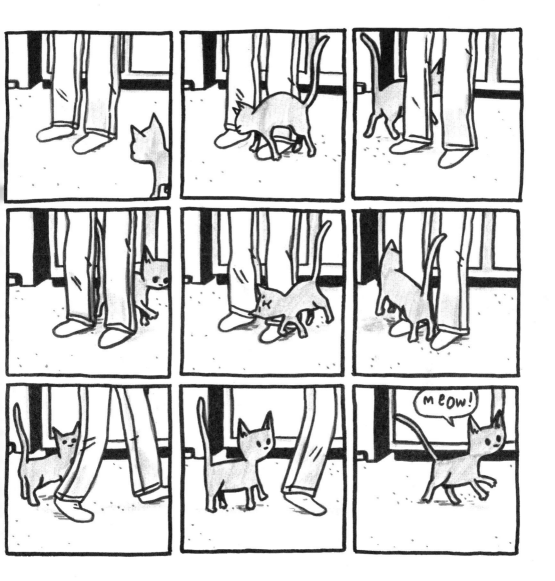

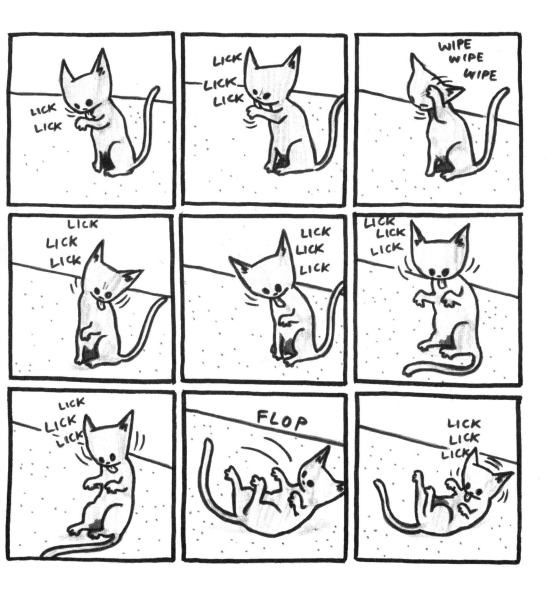

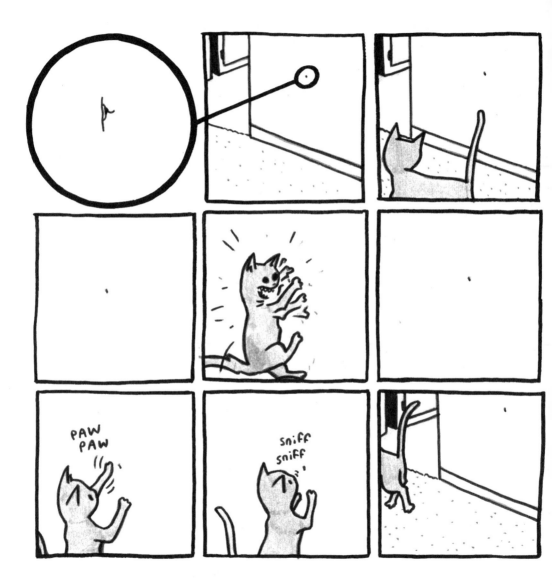

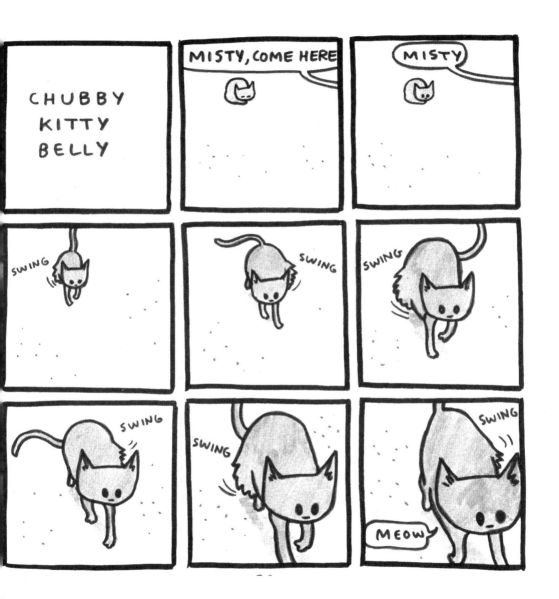

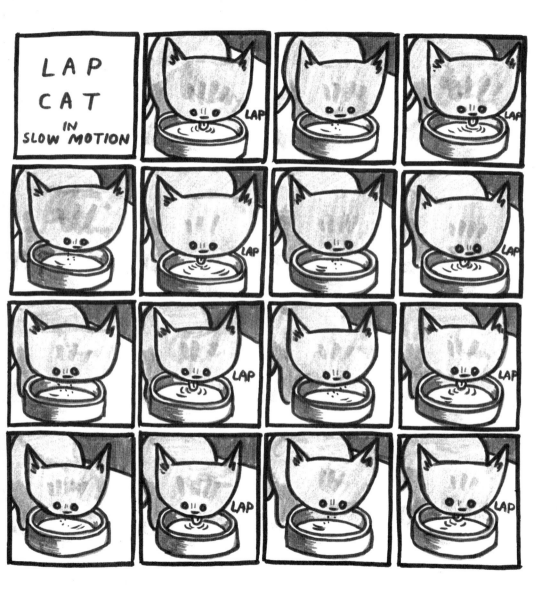

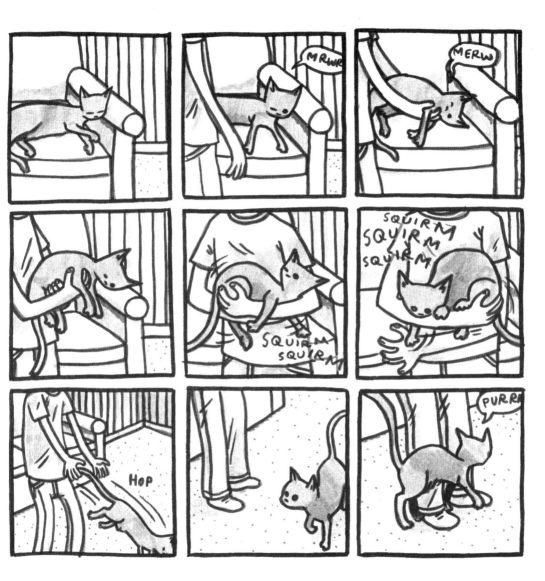

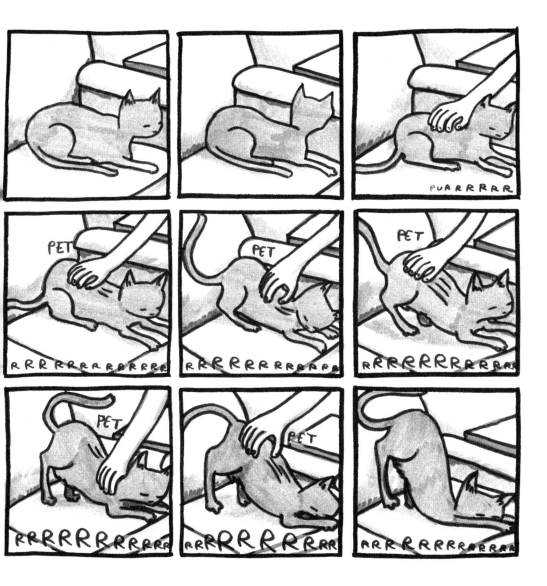

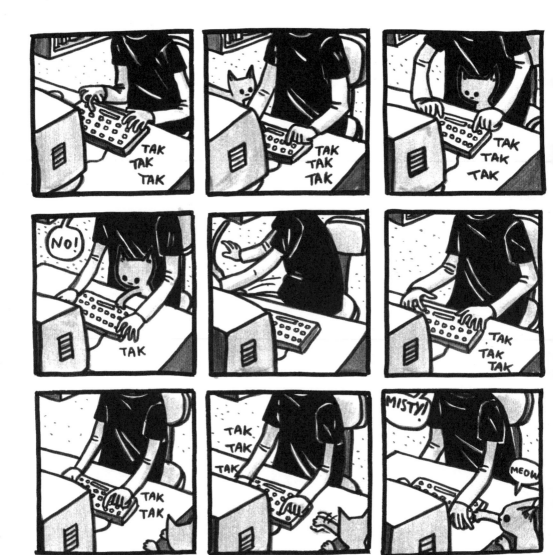

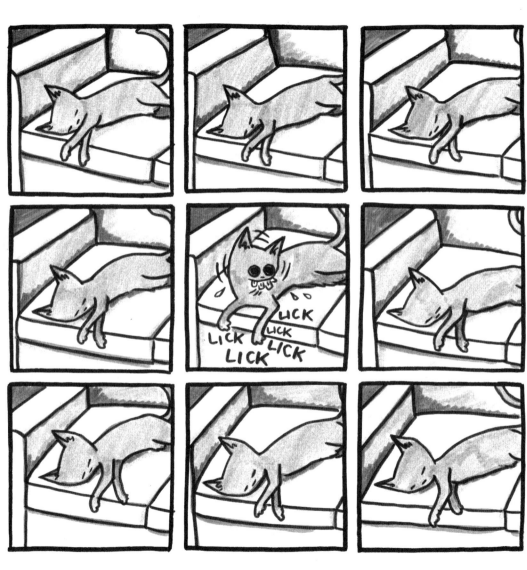

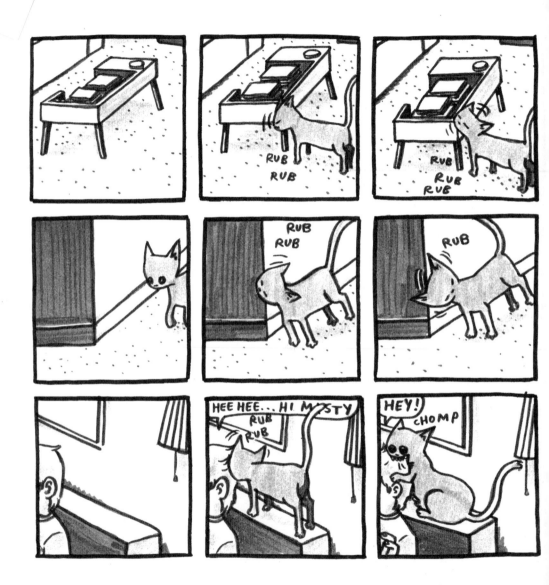

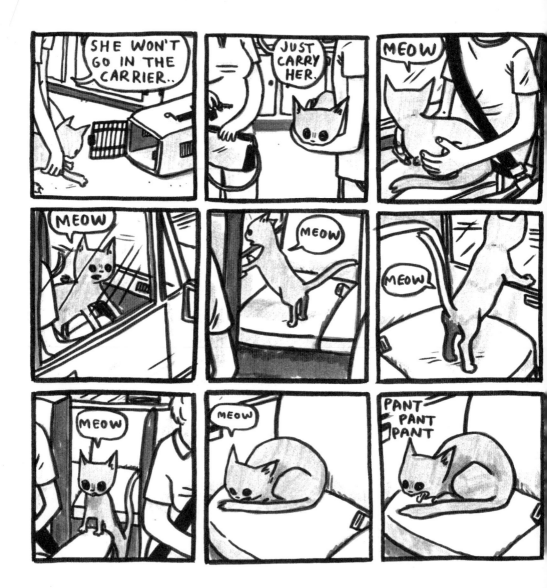

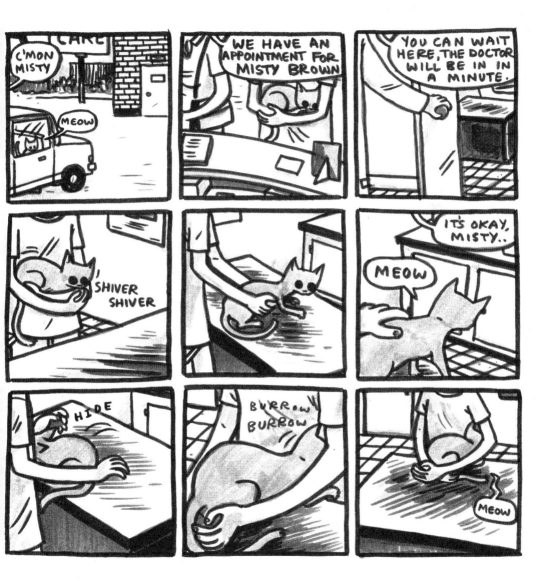

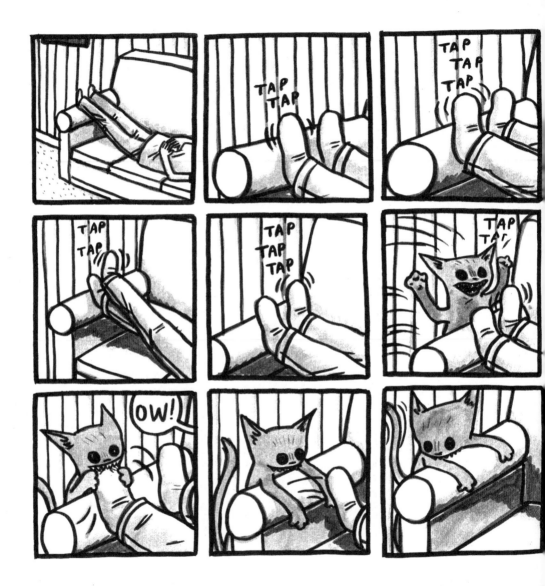

SWIPE

FLOP

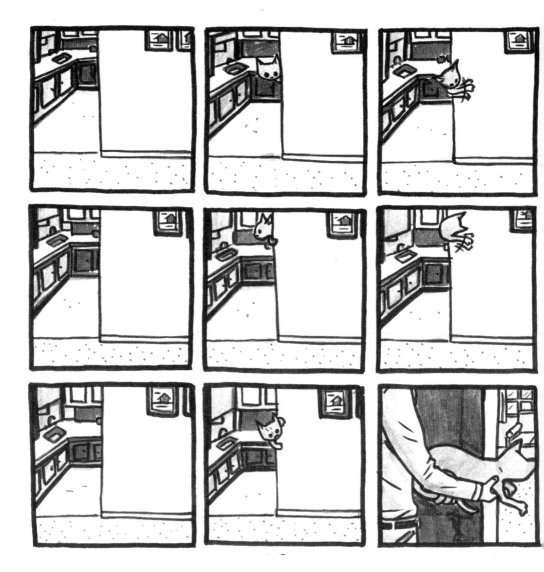

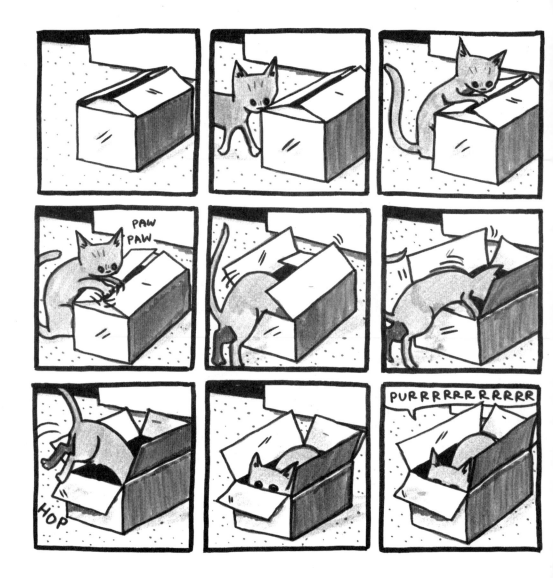

 Jeffrey Brown is a Chicago cartoonist best known for his autobiographical relationship graphic novels like 'Clumsy' and 'Unlikely' as well as humorous works such as 'I Am Going To Be Small' and 'Bighead.' Although he does not currently have a cat, evidence suggests he is still a cat person and is really just "between cats."

Write to Jeffrey at P.O. Box 120 Deerfield IL 60015-0120 USA
See more of his work as well as that of other great cartoonists
at www.topshelfcomix.com and www.theholyconsumption.com

THANK YOU

to all my family, friends and fans, especially Jennifer, Mom and Dad, Doug, Steve, Paul Hornscheiemer, Chris Ware, Chris and Brett from TopShelf, Rebecca Rakstad from RarRar Press, Kip Jacobson and Steve Mockus from Chronicle, and extra special thanks to Buddy.